A Guide to Make Knots for Kids

25+ Fun Activities to Learn How to Tie Knots-Reef, Clove, Sheet, Bend and Slip Knots

by

Jenella Bray

MA Publishers

About the Author

Jenella Bray is an experienced explorer who has a flair for untangling knots. Jenella comes from a long line of sailors, and she has spent her life learning and perfecting the art of knot tying, which she now shares with others. Her book, "A Guide to Make Knots for Kids" demonstrates that she has an in-depth familiarity with knots and their many applications. Jenella's knowledge enables readers to understand knots, use them successfully, and elegantly release their intertwined intricacies with straightforward directions and a hint of history. Whether you're an adventurer, a hobbyist, or just someone looking to improve your life, Jenella's advice will help you tie the perfect knot every time.

Author's Goal: to take the mystery out of knots, so that the reader may confidently tie them, understand their functions, and untie them with ease once the job is done.

Contents

Instructions to Use this Book

Hey there, Parents

Learning to tie knots with your child is a great way to spend quality time together while giving them useful skills. If you want to take the best of the opportunity while ensuring your kid is safe as they learn this age-old skill, this book is for you.

Teaching your child to tie knots isn't only about helping them develop useful abilities; it's also an opportunity to practice patience, cooperation, and imagination. It's important to accept both the annoyance and the delight of learning. You'll make memories and learn skills that will last a lifetime. Here are a few advices to follow to make the most of this book.

Take it Easy

Try the Square Knot or Bowline as a first knot; they are both very simple. Introduce the knots gradually, ensuring your child understands each one before continuing.

Prioritize Risk Prevention

Always stress the need for caution when tying knots. Instruct your child that tying knots correctly helps avoid mishaps and keeps objects from coming unsecured.

Practice Makes Perfect

Make sure there is a lot of practical experience. To practice the knots in a realistic setting, use things like shoelaces or scraps of rope.

Be Patient and Supportive

Know that mastery does not come overnight. Even if your child is unsuccessful on their first try, it's still important to acknowledge their efforts and remind them that practice creates perfection.

Have fun tying knots!

Yours in Knots and Laughter,

Jenelle Bray

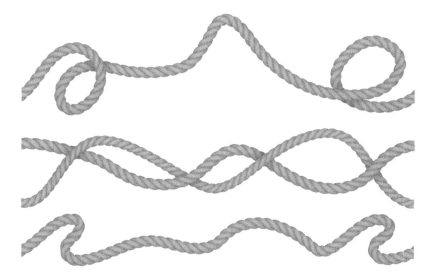

Chapter 1: All About Knots!

Get ready for a learning and exploring adventure as we explore the fascinating world of knot tying, a useful and fun skill to master!

1.1 Exploring Knot Tying Skill

Tying a rope, cord, or string through a knot increases its security and strength. *The number of possible knots that can be tied are numerous, and each knot serves a unique function and provides additional strength.* Different knots also led to some important inventions and technological advances.

The ability to tie ropes provides multiple options. A knot can be considered a unique technique to create loop, turn, and twist a piece of rope.

Learning to tie knots requires more than brute strength; it also requires a creative approach to problem-solving. You'll become a problem-solving wizard by learning which knot will save the day.

1.2 History of Knot Tying

Knowledge of knots is deep-rooted in the human history, representing both inventiveness and practicality. *Our forefathers used knots to fasten down the shelter, create tools, and tackle dangerous situations.* Prehistoric humans used basic knots for fishing, hunting, and making crude tools.

Knots increased in intricacy and functionality with time. Ancient sailors used complex knots to control the propellers of their boats in the open waters. At the time, tying knots was considered an art rather than a useful skill. Artisans' intricate knot work on garments, buildings, and books was also a testament to this talent.

1.3 Importance of Knot Tying

Knot-tying is one of the most useful and transferable skills you can acquire. This age-old talent has many useful applications and helps cultivate important traits. Some of these have been provided here:

- *Knot tying skill provides additional protection in many settings. Knowing how to tie the appropriate knots increases safety factor during camping, anchoring equipment, or responding to emergencies.*

- *It can transform you into a better problem solver. Figuring out which knot is best for a given application in terms of durability, rigidity, and simplicity in untying is a mental exercise and alertness. This is a great way to foster analytical thinking and improve judgment.*

- *Learning to tie knots is a great way to develop your imagination. You'll see their usefulness in various situations as you learn to tie more complicated knots. Ropes, with a little ingenuity and creativity, can be fashioned into useful tools, ornamental structures, and even entire constructions.*

- *The act of tying a knot also links us to generations past. Knots have been passed down through the generations for ages, and many carry significant cultural meanings. By keeping these knots alive in your heads, you may stay connected to the know-how of your forefathers.*

- *It is a great way to boost confidence and independence. Kids learn to solve problems independently using simple tools and materials, promoting autonomy and boosting confidence.*

- *Learning to tie knots is like gaining tools for various situations, increasing one's sense of security, competence in solving problems, originality, and confidence.*

1.4 Applications of Knots

Their numerous applications demonstrate the versatility and usefulness of knots. Ten great uses for knots are listed below:

Campsites and Other Outdoor Recreation: Tents, tarps, hammocks, and makeshift shelters rely on knots for installation and maintenance.

To Sail or Navigate by Boat: The bowline knot, among others, is used in lifesaving procedures by sailors to hold sails, anchor boats to posts, and make mooring cycles.

Fishing: To keep their hooks, enticements, and pivots securely attached to their fishing lines, fishermen make knots.

Climbing Rocks: The figure-eight knot is used by climbers to secure themselves to ropes and equipment for ascending and descending.

Rescue Operations: Making makeshift harnesses, lifting equipment, and anchors with knots is crucial in rescue operations. This allows rescuers to securely extricate victims from potentially dangerous circumstances.

Emergency Medical Care: Some knots are employed for securing dressings and splinting, while others are utilized in critical circumstances to stop bleeding with a ligature.

Security and Well-being: If you find yourself in an emergency, knowing how to tie useful knots like the bowline and clove knot will greatly increase your chances of staying safe and securing your belongings.

Home Responsibilities: Useful knots include securing cargo on rooftop racks, securing vehicle payloads, and constructing handles out of rope.

1.5 Basic Terms to Know

Although the vocabulary surrounding knots is vast, the following words will prove useful as you learn knot-tying skills:

Line: Material being handled with, typically, a rope or string.

Hitch: A knot fastened to a support such as a hook or a pole.

Bend: A knot used to unite two lines.

Loop: A line that loops back on itself to create a circle that is closed.

Standing End: The vacant endpoint of a line.

Working End: The tip of the line that is being tugged on or pushed to create the knot.

Lashing: A technique for joining several sticks or ropes collectively.

Whipping: Connecting a line's tip with another, thinner line to prevent fraying.

1.6 Basic Useful Knots

There are many different types of knots, but the following are a few that every kid should know.

The Square Knot

The square knot is a common example of an end knot, and so it is one of the simplest knots possible. This knot works well for securing parcels and bundles. It can swiftly secure a dressing over a wound and stem the blood flow in emergencies. In heavy winds, sailors would use a square knot to "reef" their travels or tie down a section of the sail.

Square Knot

The Bowline Knot

The bowline knot is an essential knot to know in the event of an emergency while camping or hiking. A bowline knot can save your life in various emergencies, including mountaineering, firefighting, and swimming.

Bowline

The Sheet Bend

When joining ropes of various kinds, the sheet bend knot is employed. The opening of one rope is wrapped around the other's loop to form this knot. In the past, it was commonly

Sheet Bend

used to keep a sail in place. The sheet referred to the name for the rope used to secure the sail, and the act of creating this knot was known as "bending" the sheet.

The Clove Hitch

The clove hitch is a versatile revolutionary knot for beginning and ending lashings. Lashings are bundles of rods or poles secured with rope, string, or cord. Lashings are a versatile camping tool that may be used as anything from a rack for towels to a desk to a building.

Clove Hitch

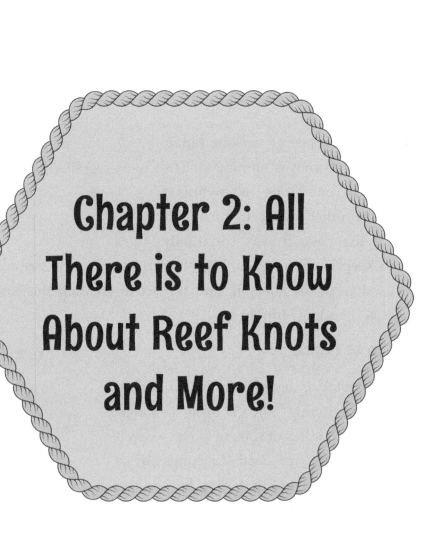

Chapter 2: All There is to Know About Reef Knots and More!

Whether you must tie your shoelaces or ropes at a base camp, this chapter has covered all. From tying reef knots to surgeon's knots, there is so much more to explore.

Get a hold of some ropes and be prepared to become a knot-tying master!

2.1 Reef Knot

Reef knots, or square knots, are basic binding knots that can tie a rope or line tightly around an item. It is also known as a Hercules knot at times. The term "reef knot" dates back to no later than

Square (Reef) Knot

1794 and refers to reefing sails or tying down a portion of a sail to reduce its surface area in powerful winds.

Uses

Sailors use a Reef knot, which has a wide variety of other uses as well. Some of them are listed below:

- *The reef knot is a beautiful way to finish off a present. To give packages a polished look, apply it to tie ribbons around the edges or secure tissue paper.*

- *A reef is used to cure wounds. It is believed that if medicines are applied to the wounds with a reef knot, they will heal quicker.*

- *A reef knot can be a makeshift belt if you don't have one. Make sure the knot is tight enough, though.*

Step-By-Step Method

The steps to tie a reef knot are as follows.

Connect the ends of a single rope by crossing the right across the left, as shown in the pic below.

Make a half loop and observe that the intertwined knots separate in a circular loop towards the right.

Reconnect both finishes; however, at this point, turn left across the right.

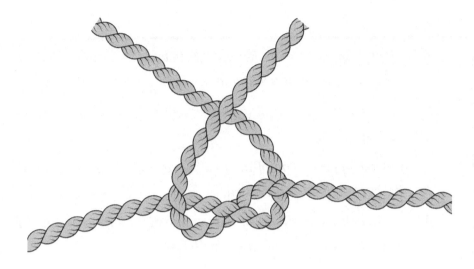

Make another half knot. Remember that both intertwined pieces spiral clockwise towards the left, which is the reverse side of the halved knot.

Untying the Reef Knot

Untying a Reef knot is easy; follow these steps, and you can untie the reef knot.

1. *Identify the sources of the rope's both ends. Remember that one approaches from the right and the other from the left.*

2. *You may form an opening with a light tug where the right end overlaps the left.*

3. *Get the opposite end of the rope by running your hand inside the opening you just created.*

4. *To switch the positions of the left and right ends, pass the left one into the loop's opening from below.*

5. *Grab both ends and draw apart slowly and carefully. The knot will gradually begin to untie itself.*

6. *After undoing the knot's sides, tug on both ends to separate them.*

2.2 Thief Knot

The unrestricted or sharp ends of the thief's knot reside on the reverse corners from those of the reef knot. The thief knot is supposed to have been used by sailors to tie up their possessions in ditty bags, frequently covering both ends. The bread bag  knot is another name for the thief knot. It resembles the reef knot in appearance. However, it has one significant and hardly perceptible distinction. It doesn't have a pair of half knots in it.

Uses

The Thief knot has become popular because of its ability to quickly change into a stronger knot. Some of the uses of this knot are as follows:

- *Magicians and illusionists frequently employ the thief knot as an element of their feats to make something seem firmly bound before they magically unwind by giving a quick tug.*

- *Artists and artisans can use the thief knot to create a sense of mystery or hidden significance in their creations.*

- *Travelers can use the thief knot to make their possessions safe.*

Step-By-Step Method

The steps to tie a thief knot are as follows.

7. Get the one (blue) rope's end inside the other (red) one's hole.

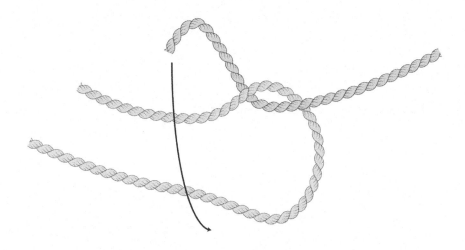

8. Afterward, get it out of the bottom of the loop.

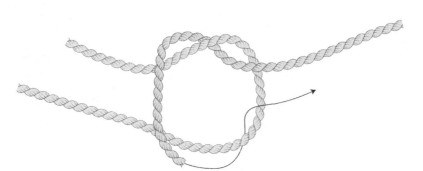

9. Pull to get a tight fitting.

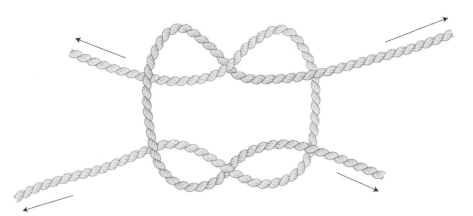

10. You now have your thief knot.

Untying the Thief Knot

Untying a thief knot is tricky, but you can easily untie it if you follow the steps below.

1. *Pull loose strands to undo the knot as much as you can. This alone may be needed to get it loose in certain cases.*

2. *However, if you still do not succeed in untying the knot, uncross the ends to release it. Keep the knot from getting any tighter by holding it gently with one hand.*

3. *Next, slip the working end beneath the other one. By doing so, the two ends will be effectively switched.*

4. *Strengthen the opposite working end by gently pulling on the two ends of the knot.*

5. *Carefully unravel the knot, paying special attention to any areas where you see tangles or twists.*

6. *It may be necessary to undo the knot several times before it is completely loose.*

2.3 Granny Knot

The granny knot is a combination knot in the knot theory formed by adding together 2 trefoil knots. Similarly, the square knot can be considered the linked addition of two trefoils, and the two are extremely similar.

Granny Knot

Uses

The Granny knot is utilized more for its unique appearance than its practicality or safety.

Some of the uses of the Granny knot are as follows:

- *The Granny knot is a great example when teaching young children how to tie knots for play. In addition, it is used to instruct young people in the finer points of knitting and other crafts.*

- *When a bandage is needed, the Granny knot can be utilized. The knot is highly recommended in these scenarios because it can be tied quickly and easily without much concentration.*

- *As an alternative to glue or staples, the Granny knot can hold something in place.*

Step-By-Step Method

The steps to tie a Granny knot are as follows.

1. Grab the separated sides of the ropes and bring them together.

2. Cross the left rope over the right one like tying an overhand knot.

3. Take the loose sides of the ropes and pull them together.

4. Cross the left rope over the right one.

5. Once you've done that, tug on the two ends to ensure that it's secure.

Untying the Granny Knot

The Granny knot is quite easy to untie if you follow these steps:

1. *To undo the knot, grab any loose rope and pull. Sometimes this is all that's required to finally free it.*

2. *However, if it does not work, all you must do to undo the knot is untying the two ends. Hold the knot loosely with one hand to prevent it from tightening further.*

3. *Next, tuck the working end under the remaining one. Both ends will be efficiently exchanged in this manner.*

4. *Take both ends of the knot firmly to strengthen the contrary, working end.*

5. *Untangle the knot carefully, giving extra attention to any twisted or tangled spots.*

6. *The knot may require multiple attempts to undo before it can be loosened fully.*

2.4 Shoelace Knot

Laces for shoes and bowstrings are typically tied using the shoelace knot, also known as the bow knot. Due to the frequency with which shoelaces are tied and untied, the knot must be simple. Complex knots may cause unnecessary stress and delay.

Uses

The fundamental function of a shoelace knot is to keep the laces from coming undone. However, there are many other uses for a shoelace knot. Some of them are given below.

- *The shoelace knot can be used as a decorative element in many crafts.*
- *Shoelace knots can replace missing or broken straps or cables to temporarily hold things together.*
- *Tents, shelters, and other camping supplies can all be secured with the help of a shoelace knot. They're also handy for attaching various items to one's hip belt or backpack.*

Step-By-Step Method

The steps of tying a shoelace knot are given below:

1. Take two laces of different colors (as shown in the picture). Start with a standard left-to-right knot.

2. You may easily make a "loop" by doubling the blue end back on itself.

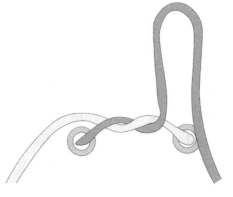

3. To complete the right loop, grab the left (yellow) side and bring it over behind the right one.

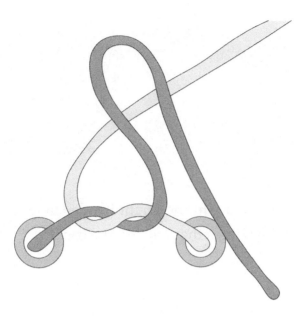

4. Move the yellow end from the left through the right loop until you reach the start of the loop.

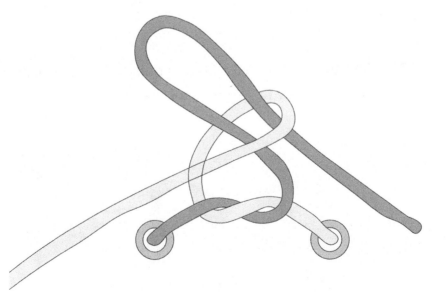

5. Continuing at the "hole" you just created, insert the left (yellow) lace.

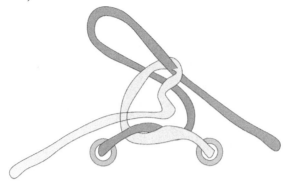

6. The yellow lace forms a right-handed loop after emerging from the hole in the center of the back.

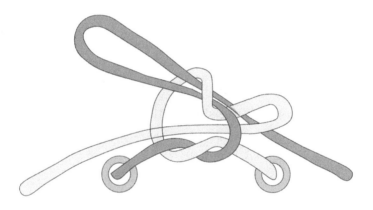

7. Get a grip on the two ends and pull them together to tie a knot. You now have your shoelace knot.

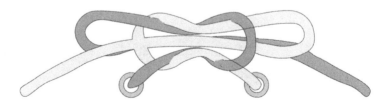

Untying the Shoelace Knot

Untying the shoelace knot is the simplest of all. Follow the steps below and learn how to untie it.

> 1. *Look closely at the shoelace knot and find the two loops that make up the "bunny ears." You pulled these loops at the end of your shoelaces to make the knot more secure.*
>
> 2. *Hold any one of the loops with the tips of your fingers and thumbs with just one hand.*
>
> 3. *Pull the other loop around your thumb and fingers of the free hand.*
>
> 4. *Separate the two loops by carefully pulling them in opposing directions. As you do so, the knot should begin to relax.*
>
> 5. *You may undo the knot and untie your shoes by repeatedly tugging apart the loops until the knot is completely untied.*

2.5 Surgeon's Knot

Surgeon's Knot

The surgeon's knot, used in surgery, is a slight variation on the reef knot. When tied, it creates an additional overhand knot at its initial toss. As the second part of the knot is being made, the extra turn might increase friction and slow down the untying process. The name of this knot comes from its frequent use by surgeons when tension must be kept on a stitch.

Uses

The Surgeon's knot is useful in many situations because it connects two objects strongly. Some of the uses are as follows:

- *The surgeon's knot is used to finish off stitches or ligaments in the operating room. It offers a strong knot that won't unravel under pressure, minimizing the risk of difficulties after surgery.*

- *Fishermen frequently employ the surgeon's knot when joining multiple fishing lines, whether the same or with distinct diameters.*

- *The surgeon's knot is useful in jewelry manufacturing, particularly when working with beads since it allows for secure and neat cord or thread joining.*

Step-By-Step Method

Here are the steps to tie a surgeon's knot.

1. Take two ropes of different colors (as shown in the pic). Position the blue colored rope across the white rope using your left thumb.

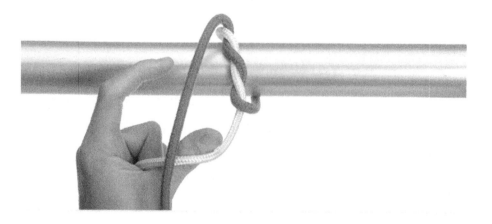

2. Underneath the white rope, slide your left index and thumb.

3. Keep the blue rope in between your left index and thumb.

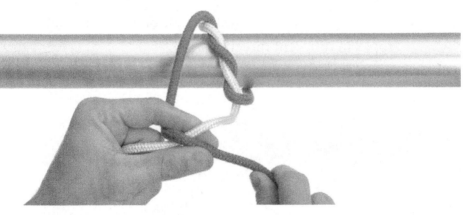

4. Move the blue rope under the white rope with your left thumb.

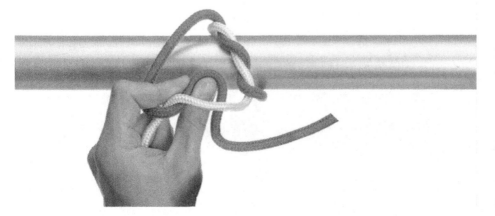

5. It would be best if you now were holding the blue rope in your right hand after passing the remaining part beneath the white one.

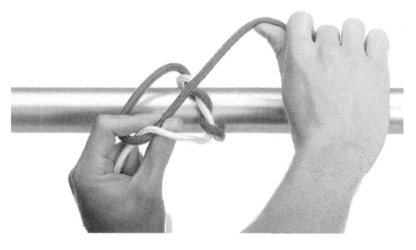

6. Turn your hands around to pull on the white and blue ropes in different directions.

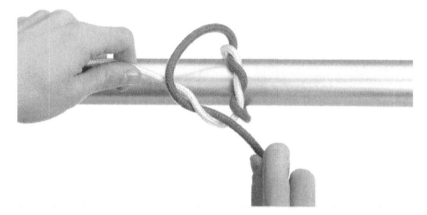

You have now tied a surgeon's knot.

Untying a Surgeon's Knot

Due to its complexity, loosening a surgeon's knot can be more challenging than loosening a regular knot, but it is by following these simple steps:

1. *Carefully yank on both ends to undo the knot as much as possible. If the knot seems too tight, try jiggling it gently.*

2. *Surgeon's knots are dual overhead knots, so untying them requires the same movements as they were tied. First, you must determine which part was draped over and which was pulled under.*

3. *Locate the part looped over initially and tug on it to loosen the overhead knot. If the knot is particularly tight, pulling too forcefully will complicate the situation.*

4. *The surgeon's knot ought to appear like a simple overhead knot once the initial overhead knot has been undone. Find the point looped under the initial one and pull carefully to undo the following overhead knot.*

5. *Even after undoing two overhead knots, the rope may still be somewhat twisted. If the rope is twisted or tangled, unwind it by pushing lightly on the two ends. In this way, you can untie the surgeon's knot.*

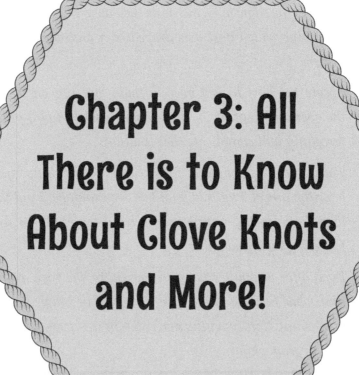

Chapter 3: All There is to Know About Clove Knots and More!

Mastering the evergreen knot-tying skill will open up countless doors for you. Learning to tie knots is like unlocking a door to a world of possibilities for development, invention, and discovery. Imagine yourself capable of building defenses, protecting valuables, and guarding the outdoors. Now is the time to round up some rope and prepare for a knot-tying journey that will mold you into a genuine little adventurer!

This chapter has covered everything from clove to cow hitch knot and much more! So let's get moving!

3.1 Clove Hitch Knot

The Clove Hitch is an old knot shape consisting of a pair of solitary hitches knotted in sequence across a given object. Even though it has multiple uses, the half-hitch is not very reliable whether applied as a binding knot or a regular hitch. It is among the three most significant knots, like the bowline and the sheet bend.

Clove Hitch

Uses

The Clove Hitch knot is versatile because of its easy construction and the fact that it may be used to fasten something to a pole or post. It is usually employed in the following situations:

- *It's a common camping knot to keep tent wires tight while anchoring on poles or trunks. It is also used to create hammocks and shelters.*

- *Sailors employ the clove hitch to secure bumpers to the side railing of their vessel for extra safety and comfort while docking. It's also effective for making quick fixes to lines and rigs.*

- *When tying a rope to a hook or other anchoring point, the clove hitch is a frequent knot employed by climbers. It's a standard component of many paragliding and belaying setups.*

Step-By-Step Method

The steps to tie a clove hitch knot are as follows:

1. Place the rope on the structure.

2. Wrap the rope's tip around the structure for support.

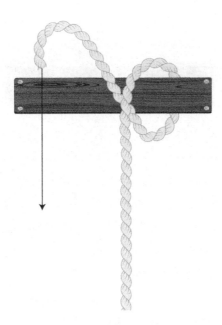

Make the handoff from the other side of the rope.

3. Pull in both ropes for a more secure fit.

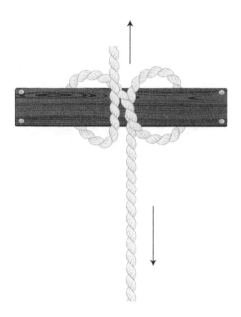

4. You now have a clove hitch knot.

Untying a Clove Hitch Knot

Untying a tied knot using a clove hitch is usually relatively easy. Untying it can be done as follows:

1. *You can slowly separate the ties that make up the clove hitch by tugging on the working end. If the knot is already under stress, you may remove the stress by drawing the rope out of the load it was securing before you tied the knot.*

2. *After the ties have been loosened, you should twist each knot loop so that they are wrapped around the thing to which it is tied. This will assist in beginning the process of separating the knot.*

3. *To complete the process, continue untying the clove hitch with a single loop at each stage. While grasping the stationary end of the rope, you should slowly draw the working end from the loop.*

4. *Repeat steps one through three for the second loop once the first loop has been released.*

5. *After releasing the clove hitch, the rope may occasionally develop a few tiny twists or knots. If they do, you'll need to disentangle them carefully.*

3.2 Barrel Hitch Knot

The barrel hitch knot, often called a barrel sling knot, represents a method of tying a loop that may be tightened or loosened as needed. Since the knot can be tied and untied quickly and easily, it is frequently used to tie down cargo, make customizable loops, and secure objects.

Uses

The Barrel Hitch knot is a staple of camping, sailing, and rock climbing, among other outdoor pursuits. The barrel hitch knot is used in the following scenarios:

- *Cargo and machinery in vehicles, containers, and ships are frequently secured with the barrel hitch knot. The load may be quickly tightened and secured using the adjustable loop.*

- *This knot is used for tying guy hooks to tents or tarps so that the tension may be changed quickly and easily to maintain the structure.*

- *When boating, the barrel hitch knot is handy for securing ropes to anchors or railings since it can be quickly loosened or tightened to account for varying water levels.*

Step-By-Step Method

Here are the steps to tie a barrel hitch knot.

1. Raise the barrel by standing it on the rope.

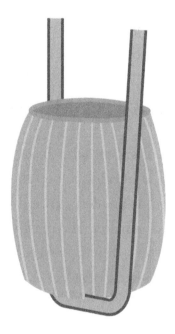

2. Make a top knot using an overhand grip.

3. The overhand knot needs to be opened so it may slide across the barrel's edges. Focus on the uppermost portion of the barrel.

4. Next, link the two sides of the rope by tying a Bowline Knot.Y

5. You now have a Barrel Hitch knot.

Untying a Barrel Hitch Knot

Here are some easy steps to untie a barrel hitch knot.

1. *It would help if you first released the wraps by tugging lightly on the working end to undo a barrel hitch knot. It's normal for the wrappings to loosen and slip.*

2. *Gently draw the working end from the hole once the wraps have been undone. The wrappings should keep sliding and unraveling as you go along.*

3. *The knot must be loosened, so keep pushing on the working end. If the knot was particularly secure, further effort may be required to undo the wraps.*

4. *If the rope got twisted or kinked when you unfastened the knot, you should straighten it out.*

3.3 Cow Hitch

The cow hitch, or lark's head knot, is a basic and adaptable knot for securing a rope around an immovable object like a ring, pole, or bar. Its versatility and ease of use make it a go-to material for outdoor pursuits, DIY projects, and general use. The cow hitch makes a tight loop over the item, and because it's flexible, you may easily move it around.

Uses

Cow hitch knots are useful because they are simple to tie and untie. The Cow Hitch is frequently used in the following situations:

- *Hammocks can be quickly put up and taken down using the cow hitch to secure both sides of the hammock with branches or supports.*

- *The Cow Hitch is useful for attaching objects to the exterior of a backpack, like drinking vessels or camping supplies, while trekking or going camping.*

- *It is useful in times of crisis because it may provide a makeshift handle for carrying heavy items such as barrels or boxes.*

Step-By-Step Method

Here are the steps to tie a cow hitch knot.

    1. First, you will grab the rope's free end and wrap it around the pole from behind.

2. Turn the rear end to be beyond and just to the left of its fixed end.

3. Wrap the working end across the pole or the support so it is ahead of the fixed end towards the opposite side.

4. Put the working end inside the hole by bringing it around the back of the pole or support.

5. Tighten up both of the edges. You now have a Cow Hitch Knot.

Untying a Cow Hitch Knot

Here are some easy steps to help you untie a cow hitch knot:

1. *Keep that object in place using one hand to undo a Cow Hitch wrapped to a stationary support.*

2. *As you do this, use your free hand to slowly tug on the working part of the rope underneath the Cow Hitch's hole.*

3. *The loop encircling the support will begin to unwind as you tug the working end. To untie a Cow Hitch, you must follow the instructions backward. To do so, reverse the order in which you tied the knot and loosen the working end.*

4. *Keep drawing the working end until the cow hitch knot is entirely loosened and its loop is released.*

3.4 Adjustable Grip Hitch

The adjustable grip hitch is one convenient knot for creating a safe and versatile loop at the tip of a rope. It's great for making a loop that can have its circumference expanded or contracted without any difficulty or blocking. It is an example of an "in-line" or "mid-line" hitch, meaning it can be knotted without first reaching the leading edge of the rope.

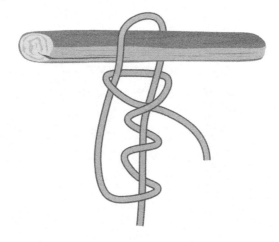

Uses

It is handy when a loop of varying sizes is required to secure an object. The Adjustable Grip Hitch is typically used for the following purposes:

- *The adjustable grip hitch can make handles, cycles, and fixings that can be adjusted in dimension or pressure for various do-it-yourself projects.*

- *The adjustable grip hitch can create belts or hooks to temporarily secure damaged recreational equipment together as an interim solution.*

- *Gardeners may utilize it to fasten plants to pillars or trees and then change the pressure as the plants expand.*

Step-By-Step Method

To tie an adjustable grip hitch, follow the steps given below.

    1. Wrap the working end over the pole or whatever you use to secure it. Maintain it next to the portion that is already upright.

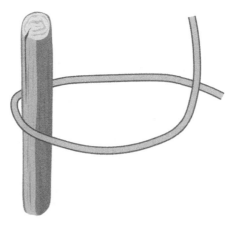

2. Double-wrap the working end all over the loop's edge.

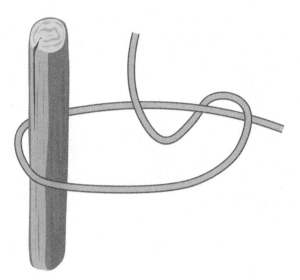

3. Next, you should drape it twice over the loop and insert the tip underneath the final loop. Tighten the knot and readjust the primary line pressure as needed.

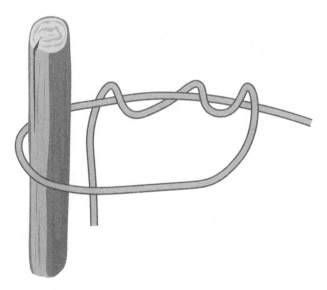

4. Form an opening alongside the working end in the final stage and pass it into the remaining wrap for a quick-release appearance.

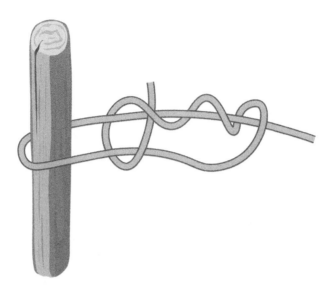

5. You now have an Adjustable Grip Hitch knot.

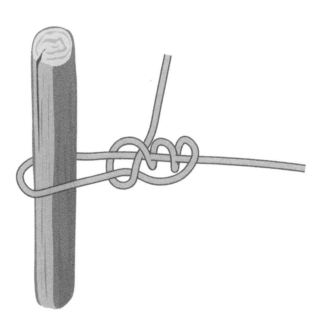

Untying an Adjustable Grip Hitch Knot

Untying the adjustable grip hitch is quite tricky but you can undo it if you follow the steps given below:

1. *Adjustable Grip Hitches are undone by sliding the loop across the standing part to progressively remove the wraps. To untangle the knot, draw the working end out of the loop towards where it wraps.*

2. *The wrappings of the freestanding section should start to unwind as you move the loop. Adjust the loop as you draw the working end to remove the remaining wraps.*

3. *The working end must be untied from the knot after removing all the wraps.*

3.5 The Halter Hitch Knot

The Halter Hitch Knot, the Lark's Head, is an easy-to-use knot for securing a rope to a stationary support like a pole, railing, or hook. The convenience of this knot in both tying and untying makes it a go-to option in many settings. It curves into a loop that slides over the free end of the rope for simple placement and realignment.

Uses

- *The Halter's Hitch knot makes a safe, adaptable loop and is frequently employed in the following situations:*

- *In horseback racing, the Halter Hitch secures a horse to a support structure like a fence or pole.*

Step- By- Step Method

The steps to tie a Halter Hitch knot are as follows:

1. Wrap the rope across the support structure (a pillar, railing, or hook). Drag the working end through the forward-most upright section.

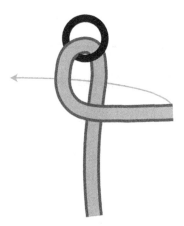

2. Then, loop back around, passing the working end behind the two halves.

3. Make an opening in the end you're working with, and feed it around the loop you just made, front-to-back.

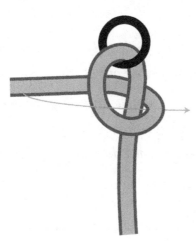

4. The Halter Hitch is complete once you give it a good tug. The loose end can be made more secure by passing it across the slipping loop.

Untying the Halter Hitch Knot

The Halter Hitch knot can be untied using these steps:

1. *To undo the knot, tug on the portion of the rope not attached to the hole.*

2. *Grasp the working end and wind it back around the hole in the same direction it came out of when you made the knot.*

3. *If you're having trouble threading the working end around the loop, try jiggling it from side to side as you pull softly. If you need extra space, slide the loop farther along the rope.*

4. *Remove each wrap by unwinding the working end to open the loop entirely.*

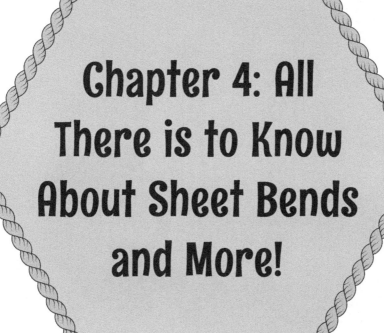

Chapter 4: All There is to Know About Sheet Bends and More!

In this exciting new realm of knot-tying adventures, ropes will become your new closest friends, and knots will give you incredible new skills. This chapter has covered you all, from the sheet bend knot to the butterfly knot and much more! These knots may sound like they belong in a fantasy realm, but they are useful life skills. You'll learn the specific steps required to tie these knots, where they might be used for fun adventures, and how to control their powers and undo them afterward. Let's begin this fantastical adventure of knot-tying, so gather your ropes and prepare to become a knot-tying hero.

4.1 Sheet Bend

When joining two ropes with distinct diameters, the Sheet Bend is a flexible and useful knot to have at your fingertips. This knot proves to be the most secure option when using ropes of varying diameters. Due to its simplicity, the Sheet Bend is frequently used to link ropes from hiking and sailing to more mundane household chores.

Uses

A sheet bend has a wide variety of applications. Some of them are given below.

- *When one rope isn't sufficiently long for the job, you can attach it to a different one with a Sheet Bend.*

- *The Sheet Bend can tie two strings or ropes together, making it ideal for DIY projects.*

- *It can join two ropes to make makeshift utility or recovery equipment in emergencies.*

Step-By-Step Method

The sheet bend knot can be tied using the following steps:

1. Take two ropes of varying strengths. The stronger rope section should be bent into a bight, while the other rope section should be kept close at hand.

2. Put the less strong rope's end into the bight.

3. Prepare to complete the knot by wrapping the less strong rope's end around the bight's head.

4. It's best to tuck the less strong rope under the stronger one.

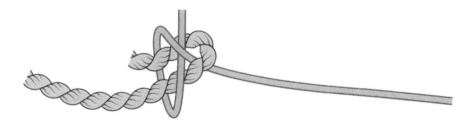

5. Now give it a good tug to ensure the knot is properly dressed. This indicates that the knot is tight and that the rope has been positioned to maximize the knot's effectiveness.

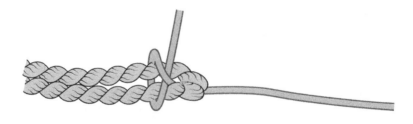

Untying the Sheet Bend Knot

Untying a sheet bend knot may feel difficult. But you can untie it by using the steps given below:

1. *Please pick up a working end and trace it to where it was originally folded within the knot.*

2. *Grasp the working end and wind it through the opening in the loop using a gentle, counterclockwise push.*

3. *Repeat the process with the second working end. Move it around the loop after winding it back from the knot.*

4. *To untangle the ropes, delicately pull them out of the hole while wiggling the working ends forward and backward. Doing so will aid in untying the knot.*

5. *Keep tugging on each end of the working rope till the knot is untied.*

4.2 The Beer Knot

The "Beer knot" is a type of knot that is often called a "Double Fisherman's knot." It is a bend knot employed to firmly bind two ropes altogether. The beer knot is a comical term employed for tying two bottles of beer jointly for transporting.

Uses

As an effective and lightweight way to link two ropes, the Beer Knot sees widespread application in adventure activities like jumping and climbing. The Beer Knot has the following uses:

- *The beer bend is a common knot to attach ropes for plummeting and climbing.*

- *Cavers frequently employ the beer bend when rigging ropes for descent and ascent in caverns.*

Step-By-Step Method

Here are the steps to tie a Beer knot.

1. In a parallel fashion, place the endpoints of two ropes.

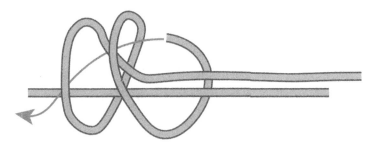

2. Wrap the excess length of one rope multiple times around the other and take it right back through each coil, then repeat with the other rope.

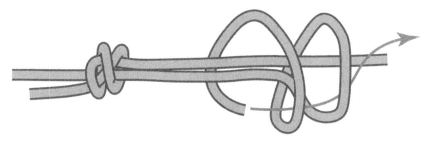

3. Switch directions and do the same with the second rope. Strengthen the knots by pulling on the loose ends, then use the standing ropes to move the ties together.

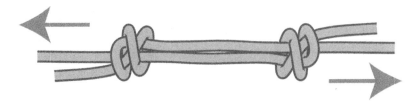

4. You now have a Beer knot.

Untying the Beer Knot

Untying a beer knot is simple and can be done by following the steps below:

1. *Release the knot by gently pulling on the working ends. If the knot doesn't untangle, try jiggling the ropes a bit.*

2. *After the knot has been eased, the two ropes should be untied. Once you untie the knot, you'll have two separate ropes.*

3. *After you've untied the knot, double-check the ropes to ensure they aren't twisted or tangled. Gently loosen the ropes to make certain they are level and usable if you come across any.*

4.3 Butterfly Bend Knot

The Butterfly Bend is a bend knot utilized for tying two ropes. It is also called the Alpine Butterfly Bend or the Lineman's Bend. The Butterfly Bend is a bend knot that results in a strong and slip-proof attachment without losing too much of the ropes' original power.

Uses

The Butterfly Bend Knot, which creates a loop in the center of a rope, is strong and adaptable. It has the following uses:

- *The Butterfly Bend is a common kite flying knot that joins the kite's thread to the harness or pulling hook. This knot ensures a firm connection that keeps the kite steady and reactive during flight.*

Step-By-Step Method

Here is the step-by-step method to tie a butterfly knot:

1. Form an eight with the rope by twisting it.

2. Wrap the upper portion of the eight downwards and around the lower portion of the eight.

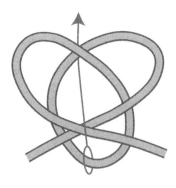

3. Now, pull the upper end into the bottom hole of the eight. You now have an Alpine Butterfly knot.

Untying the Butterfly Bend Knot

Here are the steps to untie the Alpine Butterfly knot:

1. *Start untying the knot by gently pulling on the working ends. Carefully swinging the ropes can help loosen a tight knot.*

2. *Carefully untangle the ropes after the knot has been undone. You should take your time untangling them if they're still twisted.*

3. *Keep yanking on the working ends and navigating the knot's turns. Completely undo the Butterfly Bend by unraveling it.*

4.4 The Fisherman's Knot

The Fisherman's Knot is a basic knot made by interlacing overhand knots in opposing directions. The two strands are linked invisibly and smoothly by overlapping overhead knots. On the other hand, the Double Fisherman's Knot is more difficult to tie than its simpler counterpart.

Uses

The Fisherman's knot is very famous for its wide applications. Some of the uses are as follows:

- *It is useful for joining strings or cords in jewelry, such as bracelets, chains, and earrings.*
- *It is used by professionals and amateurs alike to unite mesh lines in nets.*
- *It can secure multiple layers of cloth and stuff together as part of the quilting process.*

Step-By-Step Method

To tie the Fisherman's knot, follow the steps given below:

1. Take two ropes of varying colors (as shown in the picture). Construct a loop with the red rope and insert one end into it.

2. Use the blue rope to create a second loop and insert its end.

3. Pull on the tag edges of both knots to tighten them.

4. You can tighten the knots by pulling on the strands.

Untying a Fisherman's Knot

Here are the steps by which you can easily untie a Fisherman's knot:

1. *The knot can be untied by simply pulling on both ends. Some jiggling and light tugging may be required to loosen the knot.*

2. *Pick any loops you've made and squeeze them tightly in your fingers. Doing so will keep the knot from getting any tighter while you tackle it.*

3. *Slowly wind the rope's free end around the loop in the opposite hand. The objective is to release the overhand tie such that the loop seems to be traversed by just one strand.*

4. *After you've got one loop of the knot undone, you can move on to the other one. Keep it firmly in the palm of your hand, then, as before, feed the free end around the loop.*

5. *When both knots are undone, the rope can be gently pulled differently. Once you've undone both overhand knots in every loop, the knot will unwind effortlessly.*

4.5 Reever Knot

When two ropes need to be joined securely, the Reever Knot is the way to go. Each incoming and outgoing rope is secured at two spots within the knot, a significant feature. Because of this, it is safe and won't come free when subjected to sudden loads.

Uses

The Reever knot is employed in a wide variety of applications. Some of them are as follows:

- *Bungee jumping and rock climbing both make use of the Reever knot.*
- *In addition to that, it is also utilized in the sports of paragliding and skydiving.*
- *In emergencies, it can create makeshift harnesses or slings for carrying injured individuals, providing a quick and adjustable solution for first aid purposes.*

Step-By-Step Method

The steps to create a Reever Bend knot are as follows:

1. Take two ropes and create an underhand connection to rope A with rope B (under and over).

2. Now, repeat the same steps with the rope A. At this point, the ropes should be intertwined to form two loops.

3. Now, connect both working ends by putting the looped end of Rope B through the hole at the end of Rope A and the loop at the end of Rope A through the hole at the end of Rope B. Pull it together tightly, and this will make a Reever Bend knot.

Untying a Reever Bend Knot

Here are some easy steps to untie a Reever Bend knot:

1. *Tug the ropes on either end of the knot carefully to undo it. Allow a little stretch to work with it, but keep it tight enough.*

2. *Keep a single hand securely on the tip of the rope. Doing so will hold the knot in place while you deal with the other end part.*

3. *Locate the points wherever the ropes intersect and engage each loop with your free hand. Wiggle the ropes with your fingers to undo the original knotting motion.*

4. *The Reever Bend knot will soon be untied if you wriggle and pull the working ends.*

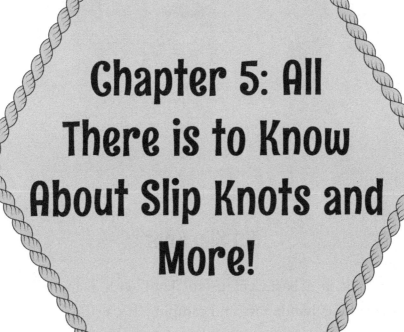

Chapter 5: All There is to Know About Slip Knots and More!

In this chapter, we will investigate fantastic, entertaining, and practical, the Slip knots. It's time to bring your knots in a row and get trained!

5.1 Slip Knot

The Slip knot is a basic yet useful knot with many applications, including fishing, handicraft, and camping. It's a simple knot that can be adjusted to make a loop to be used temporarily and then easily undone.

Uses

The Slip knot's versatility and usefulness lies in its ability to provide quick and easy security and release with the following uses:

- *In fishing, it is utilized to make loops in the line which can be tightened or loosened as required. Fishermen can modify their gear to suit a variety of fishing scenarios by securing bait, hooks, or payloads.*

Step-By-Step Method

A Slip Knot can be made by following the given steps:

1. Pick up a short length of rope.

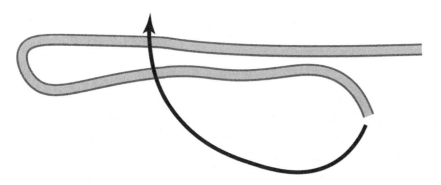

2. Tuck the tag end inside the opening.

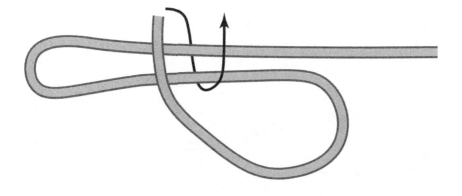

3. Proceed with the same step as the previous one.

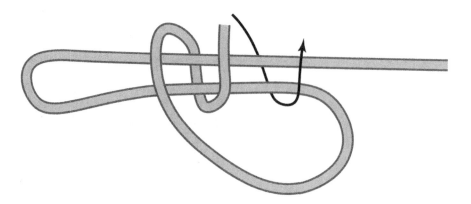

4. Tighten by grasping the loop and pulling the endpoint.

5. You now have a Slip knot.

Untying the Slip Knot

Untying a Slip knot is easy if you follow the steps below:

1. *Keep a single hand tightly on the slip knot. You'll want to keep a firm hold on it as you attempt to undo the knot.*

2. *Find the point at the end of the rope you will use. This space was used to secure the connection.*

3. *Lightly yank the working end of the rope with your free hand. When the slip knot loosens, the loop will become visible.*

4. *To enlarge the loop, tug on the working end until it opens. As you work, the knot should begin to relax.*

5. *When the loop is sufficient in size, you can draw the working end through it to undo the slip knot.*

5.2 Overhand Knot

The Overhand knot is a fundamental knot foundation for more advanced knots. To make this useful knot, you loop one end of a rope through the other end of the rope. The overhand knot is deceptively simple but is used as a building block for more complex knots and possesses several special uses.

Uses

Though the Overhand knot may appear simple, it is a major player in the field of knots. Here are some uses of the overhand knot.

- *The Overhand knot is a basic stopper knot designed to keep a rope from dangling or falling through space. It works well to prevent the ends of drawstrings and shoelaces from unraveling.*

- *It is the foundation for several more complicated knots, including the square and surgeon knots. If you know how to make an overhand knot, you already have a solid basis for learning the others.*

Step-By-Step Method

Here are the steps to tie an overhand knot:

1. Grab the tip of the rope to make a loop. The rope can be looped easily by laying one of its ends over the other. The knot is going to be situated near the bottom of the loop.

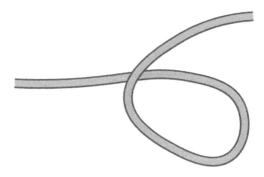

2. Insert the rope end inside the slit. Get the rope tip and insert it inside the loop while holding it together. A simple crossover and a short loop would be made.

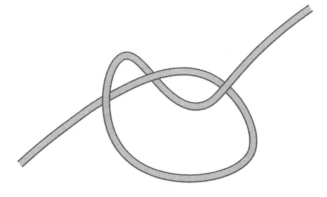

3. With one hand on the tip of the rope, tighten the knot. Take hold of the rope's tip and a few feet of it over your loop. Just draw your hands aside to quickly and effortlessly strengthen your overhead knot.

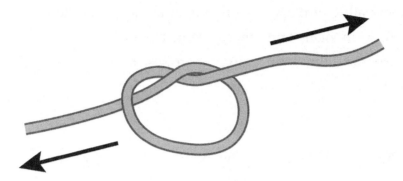

4. You now have an Overhand knot.

Untying the Overhand Knot

Follow the steps given below to easily untie an overhand knot.

1. *To undo the knot, jiggle the rope lightly on the other side. The goal is to release some tension and undo the knot.*

2. *Grab the point of the rope which isn't involved in the knot in your free hand. Loosen the knot by gently tugging the rope's tip.*

3. *The rope's looped knot should untangle as you tug on the end. Gentle pushing will unravel the loop eventually.*

4. *Once the tangle is removed, the rope may appear twisted. Just use your fingers to smooth it out.*

5.3 Trucker's Hitch Knot

The Trucker's Hitch is a strong, flexible knot that can mechanically strengthen ropes. Truckers, tourists, and those who enjoy the outdoors all love it for its convenient ability to tie down equipment and draw in neat, taut lines. Using a loop of rope and a pulley-like structure, this knot snugs up ropes, making it useful in many contexts.

Uses

Whether you're going camping, hauling, sailing, or need something to stay in place, this knot is your best friend. Here are a few applications of Trucker's Hitch knot.

- *It is an essential tool for anchoring cargo on cars or containers. It keeps freight secure while it's being transported.*
- *The ropes utilized in trellises, plant supports, and other garden stabilization purposes can be tightened with the help of this knot.*
- *It can rig up a temporary shelter in an emergency by offering taut wires to anchor tents or ponchos.*

Step-By-Step Method

The steps to tie a Trucker's Hitch are not as follows:

1. Take a rope and make a loop with it. Slide the rope into the loop.

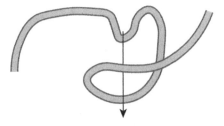

2. Keep your grip and pull to make the loop tightened.

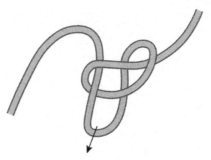

3. Move the rope tip into the loop before passing it into the hook.

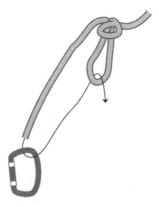

4. Tuck it into the standing end.

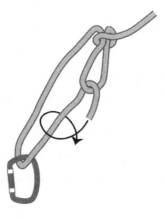

5. Repeat the same actions as in the previous step.

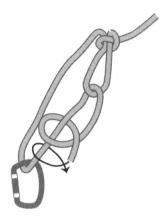

6. Pull the rope tight to get your Trucker's Hitch knot.

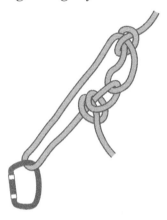

Untying the Trucker's Hitch Knot

Here are a few simple steps to untie your Trucker's Hitch knot.

1. *Figure out the hole, the Slipknot circle at the free end, and the pulley system.*

2. *Carefully tugging the rope backward in a reverse way from the pulley system will relieve the stress at the working end.*

3. *While keeping minimal pressure on the standing rope, slide the working end into the Slipknot hole (the hole made in step 2 of making the knot). The loop of the Slipknot will become looser as a result.*

4. *Carefully insert the working end into the pulley system's loop (made in the second stage of making the knot). The pulley system will unwind as a result of this.*

5. *To safely remove a loop from a load, twist the working end via it and pull.*

6. *Any extra knots or hitches utilized for securing the knot can be undone after every part has been undone. Remove any hitches or locking knots to keep the working end in place.*

5.4 Bowline Knot

The Bowline knot is simple yet useful because of its distinctive loop that cannot slide or tighten under pressure. This knot, known as the "king of knots," is essential in many situations, including yachting, climbing, and rescuing. It has been used for millennia as a standard knotting technique due to its simplicity and dependability.

Uses

The Bowline knot is a knot that can withstand the weight of a castle and can be relied on like a compass. Here are a few applications of the bowline knot:

- *Equestrians use Bowlines to make an effective loop for harnessing horses without the risk of the knot tightening and harming the animal.*

- *A loop made with the Bowline knot serves as a secure point of connection for a swing made of rope.*

- *Canoeists and Kayakers use the bowline to fasten ropes to their vessels or fashion emergency lines for use in swift water.*

Step-By-Step Method

Follow the steps given below to make a bowline knot:

1. Insert the tag point of the rope inside the loop.

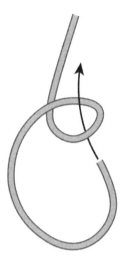

2. Slide it back into the loop and past the upright section

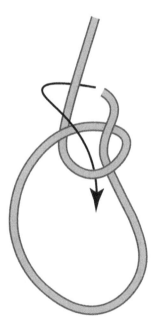

3. Get the tag end through the loop and firm it up.

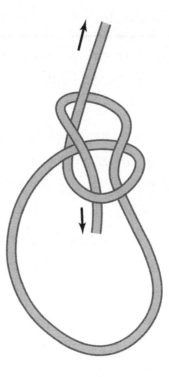

4. You now have your Bowline knot.

Untying the Bowline Knot

Untie the Bowline knot using the steps given below:

1. *To undo the knot, give the working end a light tug to release the loop. This should result in the loop becoming more open and expansive.*

2. *To undo a knot, you must pull the working end from it, then force it back into the opening reversely. If the rope is having trouble going through, try jiggling and twisting it a bit.*

3. *When you slip the working end into the opening, you do the opposite of how you tied the bowline. If you grasp the rope's working end and then tug on the upright part, the knot will unwind.*

4. *Slowly draw on the standing part while maintaining strain at the working end. If you keep pulling, the knot should untie itself.*

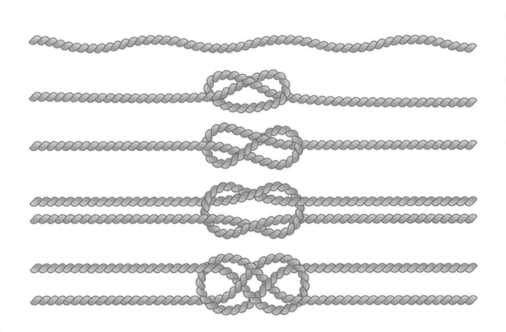

Conclusion:
So Knot Expert!

Our time together, learning to tie knots, has ended. What a thrilling trip it has been, with unexpected turns and the enchantment of finding a way to make everything fit together. As we close this book, it's worth pausing to think about how much we've gained from reading it.

Our first targets were basic knots like the Reef knot and the Surgeon's knot. Do you recall our time practicing, looping, and pulling to perfect these ingenious knots? They're like a private language spoken by all the ropes.

However, it wasn't the end of it. The universe of knots was explored further as we discovered the Figure Eight Loop and the Double Fisherman's. Each knot had a unique technique, a mini-puzzle for our fingers to work out.

Do you recall the moment we played to be Sailors and used the Clove Hitch to fasten our make-believe ship? Or when we pictured ourselves scaling peaks by tying ropes together at the Sheet Bend? As we untied the knots, we uncovered fresh opportunities for excitement.

Let's remember the value of patience as we close the book. Tying a knot requires patience and the ability to adjust your movements until the knot is secure. What about untying them? Well, it's another talent we've perfected, proving we are experts at getting things started and bringing them to a careful close.

We can do so much more fun stuff now that we know how to tie these knots. Our creativity may take us everywhere, from making unique friendship bracelets to constructing incredible forts in the wilderness.

Cheers to the closing of this book and the opening of a universe of infinite ties and unbounded imagination!

Here's wishing you a prosperous future full of knot-tying and wonderful adventures!

Made in the USA
Las Vegas, NV
01 March 2024

86590370R00050